The Last Will & Testament of My Fabric Stash

How-To Easily De-Stash, Leave A Legacy, And Make Your Fabric A Blessing, Not A Burden

1st Edition

By Jason & Cinnamon Miles

ISBN: 979-8-9939993-1-9
Paperback Edition

Published by Sew Powerful Press
Yuba City, California 95991
Cover design by the Publisher
Interior design by the Publisher

Printed in the United States of America

First Edition

Contact Information:
support@sewpowerful.org
www.sewpowerful.org

Mailing Address:
1040 Lincoln Road, Suite A #159
Yuba City, CA 95991

Corporate Relations:
dana@sewpowerful.org

Acknowledgements

We'd like to extend a huge *'thank you'* to our amazing team members Jan Cancila and Dana Buck for their help with this book project. They've both been incredible partners in the ministry, and as with so many other things, this book wouldn't have happened without their hard work, early drafts, creative ideas, and encouragement. We owe them a huge debt of gratitude – and can only imagine how many life changing donations will occur because of their support.

What People Are Saying

A thoughtful and practical guide that transforms the question, 'What will happen to my fabric stash?' into an opportunity for lasting impact. Jason and Cinnamon Miles have created something truly special—a roadmap for turning our creative collections into a legacy of hope for girls in Zambia. Every quilter and sewist should read this.

Kimberly Moos
Chief Fabric Enthusiast
Cotton Cuts

~~~~~~

When I think about God's work that Sew Powerful Is doing for a small country in Africa called Zambia, I am reminded of the Starfish moral story below. Allbrands is proud to be a sponsor! A man walking along a beach...Sees a girl moving back and forth...finds thousands of starfish on sand...Picking them one by one and throwing into sea.... Man asks her to stop the work as she can't make a difference to many of them...the girl continues saying, "It certainly made a difference to that one."

John M. Douthat
Owner & Tech
AllBrands.com

~~~~~~~~~~~~~~~~~~~~~~~~~~~~~~~~~~~~~~

Legacy is something that few people think about enough. What impact will I leave behind? How will I use my gifts to bless others? And whose lives will be better because I lived? In this book, Jason and Cinnamon challenge readers to think about these questions and present an opportunity to leave a legacy in a new and creative way.

Ashley Hufford
Personal Finance Coach
Discover Hope Financial Coaching

~~~~~~~~~~~~~~~~~~~~~~~~~~~~~~~~~~~~~~

Spending over 40 years working in the sewing machine and fabric business, I have seen numerous families going through the agony of what to do with their loved one's beloved sewing supplies and cherished stash. If you have a large coin, stamp or any valuable collection – you would make sure it has plans beyond you. Your Fabric Collection deserves the same respect.

This is a great guideline to think through what your desires are and plan for your collection. Thanks Jason & Cinnamon for making simple, practical instructions available. This will be a blessing to your loved ones as well as to Sew Powerful.

Petrina Cude
Owner
East Texas Sewing Center
Longview, Texas

~~~~~~

The Last Will and Testament of my fabric stash is a great read on how to make sure your stash is taken care of once you are gone. Sew Powerful is a great program that I have enjoyed supporting for years.

I am looking forward to adding to my will to make sure my stash is taken care of when I am no longer able to use it.

Cathy
Owner
Cathy's Creations, Home of the Ugly Thimble

∿∿∿∿∿∿∿∿∿∿∿∿∿∿∿∿∿∿∿∿∿∿∿∿∿∿∿

This book should be in every store that sells fabric. I can personally say that I am often asked, "Where should all this stuff go?" At My Sewing Room, we frequently help families find an honorable way to disperse a loved one's sewing stash. Wouldn't it be so much easier—and so much more meaningful—if we had thought of this sooner and left our loved ones some direction?

This book offers exactly that kind of guidance and inspiration. After reading it, I was moved to include a note in my own will outlining how I would like my sewing room to be shared and used after I'm gone. It's comforting to know that the tools and fabrics I've loved will continue to bring joy

and creativity to others. A thoughtful,
heartfelt, and truly necessary read for every
maker and sewist.

Anne Dale
Owner
My Sewing Room, Inc
Calgary, Alberta, Canada

~~~~~~

What an inspiration knowing my beloved
"stash" can be donated now, while I'm still
actively sewing as well as when I'm no
longer able to sew. I hadn't really thought
about de-stashing as I quilt. I love collecting
fabric almost as much as sewing itself
and I've spent years doing it. It brings me
such joy seeing the different prints on my
walls, beds and let's face it, on anything not
nailed down.

The codicil I added to my last will and
testament gives me peace of mind (and very
specific instructions), that all my lovely
fabrics will not be just tossed away but
instead be de-stashed to Sew Powerful for
use in the many outreach programs. The

purse program is my personal favorite. I've helped with several purses for this amazing project.

Jani Arnold
Past President
Heart of the Basin Quilters and Needle Arts Guild

~~~~~~

Made me Laugh, Made me Cry -WHAT? Part with these "fabric friends" I so loving chose to be close to. But this book really puts reality in place to look at the big picture of what will happen to all these things we have collected all these years. It is good to know it will help others in a positive way. Going thru my stash today!

Pati Violick
Director of Marketing
Marcus Fabrics

~~~~~~

Sew Powerful is turning a potentially hard time (cleaning out a loved one's craft space) into a beautiful opportunity to empower girls and women. Don't make your family decide what to do with your stash - read this book and learn how to do good with it!

Tara Swiger
Marketing Coordinator
SewTites

〰〰〰〰〰〰〰〰〰〰〰〰〰〰〰〰〰〰〰〰〰

This book puts into perspective the reality that many people face or will have to someday deal with. If you or if you have a loved one who has poured out their lives into a cause, steps should be taken to help continue that legacy. Have a plan for your supplies to go on and help others continue the mission. The Last Will & Testament of My Fabric Stash makes a compelling argument for their cause, but the tools here can be applied to other crafts as well.

Devin Head
Regional Sales Manager
KaiScissors.com

A Message from Your Stash

A poem by Dana Buck

"Let me introduce myself
It's me, your fabric stash
Please don't judge me bossy
Inconsiderate or brash"

"But can we have a little talk?
I think it's overdue
There's something I've been mulling that I want to share with you"

"I've enjoyed our partnership
The time has truly flown
And over all the years and years My, my, how I have grown!"

"Project after project
We've been busy, side by side
And I've admired your skill
Your creativity and pride"

"But here's my burning question One I've just been noodling on
What will happen to me
When, my friend, someday you're gone?"

"Have you got a plan?
If not, let's maybe get a jump
Make your wishes known
So I don't end up at the dump"

"It's easy with Sew Powerful
To fashion a bequest
And make your stash your legacy
To live and love and bless"

"You gathered me together
With intention, skill and care
Now madame, when the time is right
We'll still have joy to share"

"So, here's to cotton, denim
Linen, corduroy and wool
Let's designate and celebrate
And be Sew Powerful!"

Table of Contents

Introduction:

---

*"The meaning of life is to find your gift.
The purpose of life is to give it away."*

— Pablo Picasso

S ince last year, when we opened the Sew Powerful Fabric Shop in Yuba City, we've had a growing number of conversations about how people can donate fabric. People are surprised to learn we accept fabric. Many times, they're relieved — it's like a big burden has been lifted.

Sometimes these conversations are with the sewists and creator of the fabric stash. That's fun. We laugh about what they have and how much they have. Yes, we've talked to people who have 40 foot containers filled with fabric.

Other times it's with one of their loved ones, after their gone. That's much harder. It seems a growing part of our ministry has become helping family members deal with the fabric stash of dearly departed sewists. We've helped daughters, husbands, friends, guild members, and extended family members. Many times, they have no idea what's in the stash, or what to do with it. They just know their wife, or mom, or friend, would be thrilled to have the fabric go to a good cause. These encounters with sewists and their loved ones prompted us to write this simple little book. Our goal is to help you turn a fabric stash into a blessing.

We realize death and estate planning are very heavy topics, and we don't mean to be brash, make light of it, or come across as greedy. Just the opposite. Our heart is to serve and we hope this book expresses that desire – to serve our amazing sewing partners and their families, in a new and creative way. Our thrift fabric shop is ready to help.

If you decide to include any instructions regarding your sewing stash in your will - we'd encourage you to work with your Estate Planner, Attorney, or CPA. This book is not intended to be legal advice. It's just intended to prompt the question and provide a tool to use to clarify next steps.

Thank you for letting us share more about who we are, how our sewing ministry in Zambia works, and how we can work together to make a difference via your donated fabric.

With Gratitude,

Jason & Cinnamon Miles

How-to Donate Your Fabric Today

"Your legacy is every life you've touched."

-Maya Angelou

When you send your new or like-new fabric to Sew Powerful, it becomes fuel for our mission. Donations are sold in the Yuba City Fabric Shop, online, and at quilt shows. Every dollar raised goes to empower vocational efforts in Zambia. Fabric you no longer need isn't clutter; it's currency for education, empowerment, and purpose.

What We Can Accept: While we wish we could help in every situation, we can only accept

- ☐ New and like-new fabric.
- ☐ New and like-new yarn.
- ☐ New or gently used sewing supplies and notions.

What We Do Not Accept: We cannot accept everything and in particular, we don't want the following:

- ☐ Stained or otherwise damaged fabric.
- ☐ Fabric that has been in contact with pets or smoke.
- ☐ Sewn items.
- ☐ Sewing machines, embroidery machines, or sergers.
- ☐ Furniture including cutting tables, stands, etc.

How to Donate: Follow These Simple Steps:

- ☐ **Box Up Your Fabric**
  Gather your new or gently used fabric and notions. Only items in new or like-new condition are accepted. Unfortunately, machines cannot be donated at this time, but proceeds from their sale are a blessing. Consider selling them on Facebook

Marketplace or speak to a local dealer.

☐ **Complete Our Donation Form**
Visit our website and complete our "Donate Fabric" form and print out your packing slip. For a direct link, visit this webpage, or use your camera to pull it up on your phone using this QR code:

https://www.sewpowerful.org/pages/donate_fabric

☐ **Purchase a Discount Shipping Label**
Our Give-Back-Box shipping partnership will give you a discounted flat-rate label—ship up to 70 pounds to us for just $20. For multiple boxes, mark them clearly (e.g., "Box 1 of 3").

☐ **Receive Your Charitable Receipt**
Once we receive and process your donation, which must include your packing slip, you'll get a confirmation/thank-you email that serves as your tax-deductible receipt.

Using Your Stash to Make Purses

Would you rather sew for us? The process is simple. Learn more at
www.sewpowerful.org

1. Download a free purse pattern from our site and use your stash to make our cross-body purse. Include a personal note card to the girl who will receive your purse.

2. Deliver the purse to us in one of four ways:

    a. Directly mail them. Use GiveBackBox that allows (up to 70 pounds) of items to be sent to us via UPS for just $20.

b. Bring them to our booth at one of the Quilt or Sewing Shows where we exhibit. Check our website or newsletter for upcoming shows.

c. Dropped off at a local retailer collection site. There's a growing list that can be found on our website.

d. Mail to an International Purse Collector in a growing list of countries. Again, on our site.

3. Consider giving $10 per purse.

Your partnership in the ministry means a lot. We like to say *'together we are Sew Powerful'* and it's true. With your help we can do so much more than if we were working alone.

How-to Arrange A Future Donation

"What we do for ourselves dies with us. What we do for others and the world remains and is immortal."

—Albert Pike

You may hope your fabric stash makes a difference upon your passing— but unless you communicate those wishes to your loved ones, and ideally do it in writing, your family won't know how to honor your hopes and dreams.

The most important thing you can possibly do is have a conversation with your family and the executor of your will or trust. Let them know what you'd like done with your fabric stash in the future.

As mentioned, we aren't attorneys, so we'd encourage you to work with your Estate Planner, Attorney, or CPA when working to create or edit your estate plans.

If You Have A Will – Explore Adding a One-Page Codicil

If you already have a will in place, you don't need to start over. You can quickly and easily add a one-page update, known as a Codicil. It acts as a simple update to your will and is legally binding.

What Is A Codicil: A short, legal document that amends your will without rewriting the entire document. Think of it like an instruction 'sticky note' adding instructions so your family will know how you want your fabric stash handled upon your death.

A codicil can specify:

- That your fabric stash and sewing notions should be donated to Sew Powerful.
- Provide the shipping information and link to Sew Powerful's website.

- That proceeds from the sale of sewing machines or equipment should go to Sew Powerful.
- That a specific financial gift should be set aside for Sew Powerful.

Adding a codicil is straightforward:

1. Write a brief statement of your wishes.
2. Have it notarized. Places like the UPS Store offer notary services that can document your decision.
3. Store it with your will so your Executor can easily find it and share it with your family, so they can ask questions and get answers.
4. Have a conversation with your family and Executor about your wishes.

With this simple step, you can ensure your sewing legacy continues — without the need for an entirely new estate plan.

Creating a Will (If You Don't Have One Yet)

If you don't yet have a will, you're not alone — nearly 7 in 10 Americans don't. But it's easier than you may think to get one in place.

You have two main options:

- **Use a Simple Online Will Maker**
    - Tools like FreeWill.com allow you to create a legally valid will in less than 20 minutes, at no cost. There are other similar options online.
    - These services guide you step by step, even prompting you to designate charitable bequests like gifts to Sew Powerful.
    - Most platforms also let you edit your will later if circumstances change.
- **Consult with an Estate Planner**
    - For larger or more complex estates, or if you simply want peace of mind, an estate attorney is a wise choice.
    - Ask friends, family, or your church for recommendations. Or use PersonalFamilyLawyer.com

to find a qualified attorney in
your area.
- An estate planner can ensure
  every detail — including your
  wishes about your sewing
  stash.

Give Your Family the Gift of Clarity

Whether you add a codicil or create a brand-
new will, or even just have a clarifying
conversation with your loved ones about
your stash, the outcome is the same: you
give your family the gift of clarity. No
guessing, no confusion, no burden. Just a
clear path that turns your sewing stash into
a legacy of love.

Your fabric deserves a great future. You've
curated it, and when the time is right, we'd
be honored to ensure it changes lives.

What Sew Powerful Does

"You have within you the strength, the patience, and the passion to reach for the stars to change the world."

-Harriet Tubman

While many of you are probably familiar with Sew Powerful, some readers will just be learning about the organization. This brief chapter will cover the origin and impact of the organization.

Since March 23rd, 2009, Jason & Cinnamon Miles have worked to create an effective Women's Empowerment Program in Zambia that blesses students and strengthens academic outcomes.

For the first six years, they worked with eight ladies to establish a sewing cooperative to make school uniforms. It was a small passion project. But because the local ladies were terrific partners, hard workers, and very thoughtful – and because Jason and Cinnamon had a long background in Christian missions, the work began to flourish.

In 2014, the organization started working on a Girl's Empowerment Program – *The Sew Powerful Purse*. After hearing about the impact of girls staying home from school while on their periods for lack of hygiene supplies, they began to dream big. The plan was to make reusable hygiene pads there - the local moms would be paid to make the pads. Another group would be paid to make soap.

A central part of the program is to invite western donors to sew a cross body purse to help support the program. Each purse is a beautiful gift that holds the hygiene items. They are distributed in school health classes organized by the organization, in collaboration with the local schools. Each donor includes a personal note card that goes to the girl who receives the purse.

It takes $10 to assist one girl through this program, while also creating good paying jobs for the local team. That amount covers the material costs, staffing costs, and related expenses. Donors are asked to prayerfully considering donating $10 for each purse they make. It's a request, not a requirement.

In 2014 the organization collected 503 purses. The next year over 1,600. The year after that over 3,600. Then over 8,000 and the numbers have continued to climb. In 2025, the goal is to serve 35,000 girls with a Zambian team of over 60 people employed through the purse program.

In 2015 the organization began to focus on feeding children as another method of creating local jobs for local impact. Today, they feed 11,800 children daily in 26 local schools.

People have rallied to the cause from around the world. There are even 50 Sew Powerful chapters meeting locally around the country. There are purse collection sites in seven countries.

A growing number of fabric and sewing store retailers even serve as drop-off locations. The purses are all sent to the organizations headquarters in Yuba City, California, and they handle the shipping to Zambia.

Sew Powerful holds frugality as a core value and in the latest reporting period, the overhead rate was just under 3%. The 2025 budget is 2.8 million dollars and the charity watch dog agency, Candid (formerly GuideStar) has awarded the organization a Platinum rating. You can see the organization's prior year 990 in the footer of the website.

Whether you use your fabric stash to make purses today, or consider donating fabric now, or in the future, your help is a tremendous blessing.

What We Do with Donated Fabric

"To know even one life has breathed easier because you have lived. This is to have succeeded."

—Ralph Waldo Emerson

Your fabric stash is valuable — both personally and practically. It represents years of creativity, joy, and investment. It can also be donated and become a powerful tool for good.

At Sew Powerful, fabric isn't just fabric — it's fuel for our mission. Every fat quarter, yard of fabric or sewing notion can generate income that directly supports our mission.

When your stash is donated to Sew Powerful, it does more than avoid the landfill or the thrift store pile. It becomes an investment in real lives, real futures, and real hope.

How We Will Use Your Fabric & Notions

We use these donations several ways and all proceeds go to support the Sew Powerful program. Our uses include:

1. We sell fabric and notions in our fabric shop.

2. We sell the fabric at Quilt Shows. We do our best to exhibit at regional and national shows and fill our booth with fun items.

3. We sell fabric online via WhatNot: https://whatnot.com/invite/sewpowe rful

With a simple plan, you leave a powerful legacy of love.

By making arrangements now, you can remove the stress from your loved ones and ensure that your stash — whether it's a few bins or a whole sewing room — continues to bring joy and impact long after you're gone.

Your fabric has power. The question is:

"Will it end up as a burden, or as a blessing?"

Conclusion

"The sole meaning of life is to serve humanity."

—Leo Tolstoy

Thank you for caring enough to read this book. Thank you for collecting such an amazing stash filled with cherished fabric. Thank you for opening your heart to the idea of donating it to empower someone else's future.

Our hope in sharing this little book is that you'll begin to see the incredible possibilities: fabric transformed into a huge blessing for schoolgirls, fueling their dignity, hope, and the chance to stay in school. Your stash changing lives and helping us fulfill our mission.

You could have set this booklet aside. You could have told yourself, *"I'll think about it later."* But instead, you've chosen to face the hard but important questions: *What will happen to my fabric? What kind of legacy will I leave?*

Imagine it: your fabric creating dignity and hope in Zambia. We like to say, "Together we are Sew Powerful" because with your help we really can change lives. What an extraordinary gift your fabric will make.

Now, it's your turn. Plan your de-stash and send in some fabric, or write your stash's last will and testament and share it with your family.

Give your family the gift of clarity – they'll thank you for it.

If you have any questions along the way, or just want to chat with us, feel free to email us at: support@sewpowerful.org

On behalf of every girl who will stay in school because of your generosity, every seamstress in Lusaka who will have dignified work because of your foresight, and every child who will wear a beautiful uniform because of your kindness — thank you.

With deepest gratitude,

Jason & Cinnamon Miles

Codicil Template

To formally create an amendment to your will, or create one, we'd encourage you to work with your Estate Planner, Attorney, or CPA. We cannot give legal advice, but we can mention a few common tools.

What Is A Codicil: One tool that can be quickly and easily used to amend your existing will is referred to as a Codicil. Think of it like a documented, formal addition to your existing Will or Trust. We've included a sample below. On our website we have a functional PDF you can fill-in and print out. Visit us at this webpage for your example Codicil, or use your phone camera to open the page using this QR code:

https://www.sewpowerful.org/pages/donate_fabric

Example Codicil:

CODICIL TO THE LAST WILL AND TESTAMENT
of
[Full Legal Name]

I, _____
(full legal name), a resident
of _____ (city and
state), declare this to be a Codicil to my Last
Will and Testament, which is dated
the _____ **day of** _____, **20**___ .

Article I: Identification

I reaffirm my Last Will and Testament, except that I hereby amend it as set forth below.

_____

Article II: Bequest to Sew Powerful

I direct that the following gift(s) be made to **Sew Powerful**, a nonprofit organization (Federal Tax ID: 45-3327800), located at 229 Clark Avenue, suite N, Yuba City, CA 95991:

☐ My fabric stash, sewing notions, and related supplies.

☐ The proceeds from the sale of my sewing machines, sergers, embroidery machines, quilting machines, or other sewing equipment.

☐ A financial gift of $_____ (dollar amount) or _____% of my estate.

☐ Other property:

_____

It is my wish that these gifts be used to further Sew Powerful's mission of employing and empowering people.

_____

Article III: Effect

Except as specifically amended by this Codicil, I reaffirm and republish my Last Will and Testament dated the _____ **day of** _____, **20__**.

IN WITNESS WHEREOF, I have signed this Codicil on the _____ **day of** _____, **20_**, in the presence of the undersigned witnesses, who at my request and in my presence, and in the presence of each other, have subscribed their names as witnesses.

Signature of Testator: _____

Printed Name: _____

Witness #1

Signature:

_____

Printed Name:

_____

Address:

_____

Date: _____

Witness #2

Signature:

_____

Printed Name:

_____

Address:

_____

Date: _____

Contact Information & Bulk Orders

We are happy to answer questions about the content of this book. Additionally, if you're inquiring on behalf of a business, or for bulk orders, we are happy to assist you.

Contact Information:
support@sewpowerful.org
www.sewpowerful.org

Mailing Address
1040 Lincoln Road, Suite A #159
Yuba City, CA 95991

Corporate Relations Info:
dana@sewpowerful.org

About the Authors

Jason G. Miles is the co-founder of Sew Powerful. He holds a graduate degree in Business Administration with an emphasis in International Non-Profit Management, as well as undergraduate degrees in both Organizational Management and Biblical Studies.

He previously served as the Senior Vice President of Advancement at Northwest University, his alma mater. He started his career at World Vision, where he spent sixteen years in both Human Resources and Development.

Cinnamon Miles is the co-founder of Sew Powerful and Pixie Faire, (www.pixiefaire.com).

She is also the best-selling author of *The Idiot's Guide: Sewing* published with DK Publishing and *"Sewing For Beginners"* frequently found at Costco, Walmart, and bookstores worldwide. Available through Future Publishing.

Before co-founding Sew Powerful,
Cinnamon worked at World Vision and
served with YWAM (Youth With A Mission)
in Eastern Europe.

Learn more at: www.sewpowerful.org

About Sew Powerful

Sew Powerful is a Christian ministry serving in Zambia, and based in Yuba City, California. Their mantra is simple – *local employment for local impact through purposeful products.*

In Zambia they create purposeful products that change communities-things like school uniforms, reusable hygiene pads, soap, hot lunches, backyard gardens, and farm fresh food. Started as a uniform making co-op in 2009, with just eight ladies, it has grown to over 160 people at the time of this writing. They are changing Zambia for the better.

The organization has been awarded the Platinum Transparency Seal by charity watchdog group, Candid. In the most recent reporting year, the organization's overhead rate was an astonishing 3.2%.

This year the organization hopes to accomplish the following:

- ☐ Serve 36,000 girls via the Sew Powerful Purse program in Zambia.

- ☐ Manage daily feeding programs at 26 of the poorest schools in Lusaka serving 11,800 children.

- ☐ Share the good news of Jesus and Gospel Literature to 40,000 children.

- ☐ Manage 120 urban backyard gardens to assist the neediest households in the community, primarily widows and the sick.

Learn more at www.sewpowerful.org